Cactus Land

Philip Byron Oakes

77 Rogue Letters

Cactus Land by Philip Byron Oakes
Copyright © 2008 by Philip Byron Oakes

All rights reserved by the author. No part of this publication may be reproduced, stored in a retrieval system or transmitted in any form or by any means electronic, mechanical, photocopying, recording or otherwise, without the prior written permission of the author.

ISBN 978-0-578-00707-6

Printed in U.S.A

77 Rogue Letters
Austin

http://philipbyronoakes.blogspot.com/

Many thanks to the editors of those journals in which poems from this volume originally appeared:

Cricket Online Review, Euphemism, Glitter Pony, Hamilton Stone Review, Horse Less Review, My Name is Mud, Otoliths, Sawbuck, Switchback, Taiga, and *zafusy.*

For Tammi, Lara and Ryan

Contents

Ambience 6	7
The Line Between	8
Outer Skirts	9
Profanity on the Wharf	10
Amerikan Polka	11
Gray's Shawl	12
Lost and Found	13
Passage	14
Right on Roosevelt	15
Rule of Law	17
Viva	18
Dream Taxidermy	19
Earth To	20
Shadowmen	21
Today	22
Sheer Commerce	23
Nominally	24
Divination	25
As Easy As	26
Errands	27
Flight School	28
Marking the Calendar	29
Meet You at Two	30
Ex Nihilo	31
Nestor's Day Off	32
Big	33
Buridan	34
Colloquial Patter	35
Death in Life	36
Counting Around	37
Unfinished	38
Near	39
Cliff Diving	40
Fathoms	41
Keeping It	42
Cover	43
Profile Cabinet	44
Birth of Etcetera	45
Silhouettes	46
Do	47
Lean To	48
Here	49

The Air	50
Now is Here	51
Dulcet	52
Plus	53
Now and Then	54
academy	55
Simple	56
Sensible 2	57

Ambience 6

A grief of long coats skating to
the tint of bruises, on the breast
of a failed philanthropist.
Murmur's last legs as they wade
the Ganges. Not tall, stippled.
Rubicund, but no fire engine. A
lapse in the grandeur of night's
grip allotted a radius of elbows,
highlighting the shortcomings of
giants in the arena of spaces to
crawl. The aftermath of
effervescence. A connection to
the freckles of the hoi polloi. A
ballyhoo of trombones, or else a
kiss on the cheek gone awry to
seek its fortune. A place, where
the tallest of the dwarves make
the technocrats feel welcome,
where even the realists lose
count of the heartstring theories.
Reconnoitering a foot in the
grave consequences afforded
winter wear. A favorite color of
the unconscious. Before the
dawn, the apple, the thorn.
Posting bulletins on the sleeves
of forget–me–nots, fading to the
beneficence of black. Ergonomic
small talk, painting miniatures by
charlatan light.

The Line Between

The previous takes a backseat, the last
in line taking center stage,
on a bicycle built for two. Four minutes
into the smell of smoke.
Apologies carry the weight of a
generation up the stairs. Cats bark
at the coming of the Lord. Whereas
a semblance sees the old shames get buried,
before the rent balloons. A
tumultuous cuddling accounts. Tongues
recant a coo. Limpid is where the
shadows lean. The brunt to be mastered
in a slouch of pilgrims. Bossa novas,
of the clubfooted, leaving a legacy of turgid
rhythms stroking Mrs. Beasley's brow. The
thin ice of hosannas catching the
elephant man by surprise. Chinks,
in the persona, spinning bridges too far. A
long wedded wife, blowing kisses from a
miraculous driveway. The winds digress.
Blackened grays. Purity, clabbered in the
equatorial doldrums snaking their way up
the coast. Colors, coded and shrill at a
distance. Ruby lips reciting the school menu,
in the mezzo–soprano of beach bunnies
splashing away gravity's curse. A
desperate paralysis keeps the squirming
to a minimum. Severed phantoms
teaching pain. Blunted caress. Darkling
boogaloo, threshing fallow whole,
expansive, in the least.

Outer Skirts

Splicing of events growing frayed under a scrutiny of spindles. Peek–a–boo in retrospective indemnity. The glutinous remedies trickling, a parody of tears. The rudely hoisted land. Fish eyed mutineers, launching paper boat manifestoes, a silk of sayonaras godspeeding a lonesome word from the front. A run on the banks of the river. The fauve gaze, a cryptic tide of newly dirtied verbs, a plentitude of color's stooges grown gray. Elephantine, come pocket sized to the party. The fat side of someday. Blunt slickered with brilliantine, a prickly rhetoric of undercurrents turning tides to symphonic movements for change. A coterie of narcissists, voluntarily bolstering the ranks of an army of one. A wisp of atoms eroding beneath the feet of a track star. A swallowing of old angular prides, the roof of the bubble built to float, as the lizards sun on the rocks of creation to assure the children of the continuity of time.

Profanity on the Wharf

Polyglotted slur through bubbles
tickling crescendo
on the chin.
              What's that? A ferris
wheel well on its
         way to work.
   You might as well have
signed the execution order
yourself.
            The daisies are on the
ochre side of yellow.
   Appealing to better
natures keeps the ice caps
melting.
  Pickerel isn't a fish you want
to mess with. Repeal in
midstream.
It's unlikely the moon will feel
the effects
of the crash.
   The cathedrals will be open for
business.
             The kiddie pools
will be aslosh
    in fading grandeur.   The
sun will ape a beacon in the sky.

Amerikan Polka

Asthmatic rhetoric urbanely conquistador grating cheese. And then frogmen legs like Betty Grable, mottled to complement the rajah of la-di-da, no longer clicky clacking their porcelain heels. It's true. A bluster of belief in the city's faint odor of lizard droppings, wafting like a third world carnival ride, into the anticlimactic sphere of what's left of Schenectady. An oncologist plotting the arc of the covenant to breathe. The getting wet. Swimming language with loopholes. Beyond the pale of anorexic teenagers. Tinhorn anesthesiologists, promoting amphetamines at a birthday party for inclement weather; not the copilot, the time of day written on the palm of his hand, nor the unkempt cosmetician leaving elbow room for the beauty of life. The too loose to be worn in public falling into craters of suggestion. A parked car on the interstate luring Floridian playboys to yodel biblical text into the frantic naivete of early evening. Tegucigalpa and a toucan on a stick. A kamikaze refrigerator, bringing the whole house down to where the brittle people live, like like is love, and love is a house haunted with incompatible chocolates, and a passenger pigeon on the breath of an inimitable missionary wearing his hair just so.

Gray's Shawl

A teamster's melancholia steering the
truck to sobriety, in the contraflow lane
that gives the grid its whiz. Wait a minute's
life. The acid rain meeting its match, in
Mamie's potatoes au gratin; the palm
trees blinking in their pose for paradise.
Aneurysms in traffic spilling truth serum
into café au laits: the toreador wielding a
holy grail, won in a raffle to end the plague
of shallow waters lapping at the feet of
better men than that. Anointed takes a
powder in the fifth, to resolve a debt to
mystery. Sadness, you know the rest.

Lost and Found

A reprise of dodo birds,
taking one last stroll
beneath a sky of
forbidden pleasures.

Leaning into the
moment of departure, a
fanatic, in a twitch of
tranquility, juggling
crystal balls in a fog
that tells it all.

A residual hysteria, in
the eyes of a survivor,
brewing implications in a
house of cards wobbled
by the very thought.

An ephemera with
shoulders punching
holes in missing hours
on the clock, stumping
pundits with the beauty
of absentia.

Passage

An arching gape
fruited plain as Jane
Boo said the passage
was narrow into nary a
moment to spare. Eye
of the needle blinks
semaphore peeking
through gossamer
cause as affects the
yet living still. And
frightsome bullies
trundle through the
tunnel past the
gateway to the
opening of spaces
between promise and
dearth of room to run.
Colossi in the
peephole bungle the
magic living large in a
looming like a light in
the absence thereof.

Right on Roosevelt

Adenoidal eloquence dispensed
in grog of toodle–oo's. Christian
burial in dirty work absolving
tennis elbow in the door. A trail
mix of banter and brawn.
Fundament in the cleats, strode
the plank to pass act three of
congress. A popular treat in
1902. Sandwiched stood to
ridicule the saint of teflon
leanings. Muleskinner.
Refrigerated acolyte. An
extenuated leg, other foot.
Tongue sponged taffy drooler
made to think in threes. A saga.
Feeble as feasible in the
interstellar. But not here, the
people clamored. Radical
lounged. As I saw. I swam. The
gracing of participles with
nothing to wear. The versions
vary according unwanted
guests. As the immensities are
porous. A tyranny of footprints
left to wander aimlessly.
Polygamists fudging with
bombshells. A respite spelled in
looking elsewhere. Not where.
The where else can you make
your mark of Cain. If not muted
screaming tuning the piano to
the key to the city. A balm.
Another glory. A handsome
toad. The view is everything you
said it wouldn't matter.
Whether or knotted they come.
To glide over the dance floor of
who I am. Not an avenue.
Strudel tossing pig farmers
marginalizing the infinity of

inner space. Approximate consuming. But far be it. Go to it. The ponder–able prairies stippled with mugshots of pioneers, gracing wet willies of the wisp with a name so common it sleeps on the tongue of a tourist. A circuitously fastest way possible to rend a tale inert. A caught betwixt. Friction's escort. Dump and dollar down on the pony in red. The ephemera will still be here in the morning.

Rule of Law

stipulates bungled virgins
erect ironic curtains
juxtaposed in arrearage a
populace imposes
glimpses into a painted
mirror black the
taste of beans uncounted
worthy to serve a minute
with a dollar to spare
a friend
a limb of lips stuttering
countdown to to fro for
aging echoes traffic out
the door
is down
the hillock of hop to skip
the fireworks
for error's trial
applying ointment
to the physics of the day
jake saw juju
jolting jeepers
bribing linguists to say
the sun will shine for
money plenty's kin to say
it's cold wherever else
they go to hide their
faces

Viva

                                      Gelded anomalies of cartoons in the
street, gathering wits by the bushel for Labor Day. Regrettable
epiphanies clearing the fog of litter. A horse serenade fomenting
stampede in murmurs, through an audience easily
distracted by the smell of hay. Gaudy resolutions, beyond the reach of
gravity's parlor games.
The spiritually empty repository for waffles, growling the call
of the wild mayor of Borneo, living and dying on the whims
of the great apes. Requiems commandeered by kazoos,
lilting the bottom line to sleep on the launch pad of a rumba
haunting the forest with the fields. Squints upon the wide
eyed
breaking the law
of optics, into components of belief in the sight soothing
the soreness of eyes. Names sworn to secrecy as to whom
they'll shower with gifts. The freckles plaguing alabaster, in
the marble façade of prior bad acts throughout a play on
words that kill. The growing spurts of elves under
interrogation, for crimes on the top shelf of the larder of
derelict reverie. The
priapic disability allowance of a purple hearted trooper.
Codes of honorable mention.

Dream Taxidermy

Collusive mavericks, putting team on a pedestal to be eaten from the bottom up. Erosion to the rescue. Superlatives of the middle ground, leading casual observers to inevitable conclusions, watching the iceberg set sail on a whim to cool the ocean. A feature length façade of the season. The remarkable coincidences that make each fact a subject of suspicion. The going round coming home for junior's graduation. A menagerie of blasphemies, breaking glass of its habit of clarity in the argument for light. An industry of misunderstanding putting byproducts center stage, for Romeo to dance around like the pinkest of elephants in the room. Backstroking in concert, to amuse the captain of the barge, as he drifts off into the history of water. Simple oversights, compounded into discoveries of lands, amassed outside the doorstep, of eventual winners in the race to spread the news. A failed logic to the trees' dominion over Elm Street. The last supper, taken for granted the world is growing warmer to the touch. Spinning the text of a beginner's manual in the art of fading away. Karma's pendulum swaying in the sea breeze of a fashion magazine on fire. The chasm between man and dog.

Earth To

A lackluster hegemony forecasting fish on the line between east and west. The slow standing out of the way of the world, for directions seeking help from strangers. The grandeur of motes in the eye taking out billboards for a night on the town, by the river running like a free spirited convict to his epilogue. A supplemental symphony of air raid sirens, steering music back to melody's kiss of a cousin. The all too possible, factoring into the proof that nothing happened in the arms of truly yours. A subliminal mistletoe in a room of lips sewn shut. The falconer's oblong decree. The harshly extracted perfume of the misty headed, wafting unabated in assaults on the clarity of the simply said. Played at the peril of green thumbs mired in the dark and weedy fray of life.

Shadowmen

An anonymity of the innocuous, saving bells the trouble of ringing the perimeter with palm trees. Scrap iron moustaches disguising glottal stops, with stutters taking tympani to quiet time. Body's better bluster, worn in echoes of voices suspended from active duty for violating a whisper in the dark. An octopus in the jungle. An elephant in the deep blue sea. Little Mr. Invisible, sized for handcuffs in the emporium of guilty pleasures. The rudimentary collusion of events in the making taking turns. The diabolical applying for certificates of normalcy, in the amber light of postcards to the cousin who never could. The ventriloquist who never would say why.

Today

Dead harlequins making wooden Indians smile. Fortunes found in the architecture of smoke. I shutter the windows to think. The climate is such a tease. The colonization of a long silence, captions and epithets, like poodles escorted down a sidewalk losing sight of the road. The shadowy dance of gnomes, in a forest of concrete once rich with the howl of wolves. Something out of the side of Shirley Temple's mouth. Pointless fingers, making amends a joke between the pianists. The cavalry might as well have come spitting rose petals. Sequestering butterflies, for their testimony at a splash of color. An amalgam, disintegrating into Mozart, doing pushups in the right way to quiet. Pushing statues out into traffic. The hand on the shoulder of the man with his hand in the air.

Sheer Commerce

Mississippi deep as cold toes will go eight of
nine yards. A hysterical dimple. Glory's sister in
a late American chair, rocking the middle ages
to sleep where leisure time stands still. Grecian
urn your pay, or else who'll know the arid
temperature at which hearts melt to blood
liqueur. Over and over ice cream with the
shadow queen, deeply breathing her crackly
poetry of fallen leaves. The mean spirited
surrenders hostages at the altar of nakedness
in the story of Nod. As fully furnished would
have the morality play curtailed, for little
mention of the Mona Lisa prancing in the
rearview mirror. The purple truck cascades. Itty
bitter slips. Prince Valiant virtuosos, in the craft
of cheek massage, lay groundworks. Dodging
artful science beneath their feet, before
stepping onstage. Irremediably broken prima
donnas play with their ringlets as they cry.
Fixtures at the bowling alley happily parade
their prize winning shrimp sauce. Boogey
vendors stir naptime, with exotic lemon pepper,
and a manifesto of sighs funding the sails of a
sampan in the svelte harbor of contrary souls.

Nominally

Tepid laps around the obelisk, obscuring what circles can do. The graybeard's swim in a ritual of failed drownings, colloquial jest of placid waters. A limerick of tall orders, putting short people in a place they can reach. The collaboration of distance in the holding dear. A challenge to the granular quality of salt, to serve as grit in the grating collapse of an empire; a testament to the bravado of entropy, securing chaos a slot in the hall of fame. A melodrama mooted, in cutting to the chase of the lighthearted through a slaughterhouse. Troves of shadow, stalking architecture to congratulations for its performance between the lines. The casual cruelties weighing in at **600** pounds. The bluntly put to rest in nuance. The hardly noticed in its ubiquitous array.

Divination

The zealot's satire with fangs and a rose
garden at the dark end of the house with
candles. There it was. Anyone's guess. As
good, if not better yet. The rhinoceri running
unfettered through the parentheses, with
which the savannah is fenced. I meant to call
you. Sir. If the state of the obelisk is any
indication. The derelict's entourage find the
shadows accommodating. The sheets, crisp.
Violets abandoning purple in a pinch. The
march, into the belly of the megasaurus,
being complicated by the mellifluity of
tangents, spicing sidewalks with toe tickling
delights, to the amazement of incumbents to
the smell of bacon. Slumbering enthusiasts
making their stand lying down. Isn't that just
like an Etruscan? Sneaking out the front door,
at the ellipse in the discussion of the ratio of
biscuits to life spent searching for water.

As Easy As

Sullen diplomats playing Parcheesi, with lives of the abstracted to a number between zero and ten. The glue of earth and sky, distilled in the contours of a building set to music promoting the rhythms to a season of one. Four scoring plenty. Five will get you malaria, on the tundra of another day at the office, spent calibrating the hat size of presumable Livingstons taking in the ambience with an umbrella. Three rounding to the odd folktale, of expeditions from the woodwork, meant to manifest resolutions of eternal doubt as to the inching miles of true measure. Six will get nine lives lived in memory of the smell of bread unleavened, over the physics course of a factoid, cutting a farmer's swath through the greater lies of the time. As two times eight makes pristine the eventuality of a detergent, sending bubbles as emissaries in lucky sevens to the echo that counts.

Errands

Blood slush funds spilling preventable
oxygen on Saturday's swath they
quiescently leave to tour lush wooden
neighborhoods where eight of nine lives are
lived in sequestered providence of grievous
shortcomings grown laudable shoulders on
the sticky ilk of day somehow cheapened by
smudgeproof windows or not she stood her
ground in the diary of a mothball with a
semi-colon in her soup stirring soap for dirty
bellies embellished by lemon where limes
are blue in the storyteller's drawl you hear
when little if anything is ever heard of the
combustible shadows shedding human
ashes to ashes as reason why good people
suffer the seared horseflesh of a
compromise from the crosswalks between
the here of your right foot and the now of
the Fuller Brush man at the door of the
charnel house of five cent glimpses at the
golden ring me any time you see my hands
are free to squander the time it takes to
breathe

Flight School

Voodoo in the hairdo of Marie Antoinette, dark end of the cave with curtains. Push comes to see shove in its underwear. Populism of starched collars cut and dried, resonance of unsaying widows of the second wind as sashayed, a forensic limerick weaving pigtails for the blind. Contagion of stigmata in the Nabi garden, a glut of alchemies in the loafers. Cruelty of labyrinths on Easy Street, the tingly afterglow of moments stolen from beneath a veil of hiccups. The hubbub, somehow lost between the commas. That's what it means to be major general. Astral planes are grounded till the weather clears. Boogeymen take a number like everyone else. Axioms in wheelchairs are commandeered on slurring sleds of paraphrase, a lapse of manual etiquette at the door. Fleshy when wooden even so.

Marking the Calendar

Anniversaries of old news, masquerading as news of old reborn; as never having gone away the way of all birthdays, fattening up a calendar to straighten out a circle that never stops. You couldn't have painted it any prettier in pink, mauve on crutches, limping through a kaleidoscope of experience; a horn on which to blow warnings as to the capacity of the desert to roil. The millennial yawn, taken for a roar from a distance of epic inches, accounting for the vertiginous trek to the anxious succumbing. A richly constituted prayer of insufferable hubris slinking past the teeth of a certified simpleton, taking wing in the ambience, prospering at a narcissistic distance on the shelf where state secrets go to die. A chronologically challenged chain of events getting entangled in the testimony of a secret agent, ever so incrementally polluting the stream behind his house. An achingly familiar figure in an easy chair pointing at the one who got away.

Meet You at Two

Dark fantasy filibusters snarling traffic, in laggard's fast lane to a good night's sleep; Lawrence Welk's saxophone spicing silence with a drive thru yawn. Apprentice harlequins caressing gently used satin, where stuttered blasphemies unite into a practiced purr. Lacunae hide away beds. We're all just standing there, see. The stop signs equivocating for candy. An inaudible sigh in a Panama hat, the answerable quote, homesteading the tongue in summation of sticky heels dragged down the stairs with the flavor of oompah; each word hosting the mischief of sunrise on the verandah of a drawl, giving a view of downtown its chance to breathe. A character in a play on words. A window that is a wall, a look backwards, a keyhole, a whisper, binding subliminal forces to a credo of blinking nods in the maelstrom. Svelte angst easily captured, glomming whittleproof to toxic conundrums, coagulating equations, buoyant and to the breeze. A puff of smoke walking the straight line, with a limp meant to subscribe to a story.

Ex Nihilo

Confusing father's path to
mother's breadth of depth in
being there;

the ditties of the colossus dicing
background, to complement the
fall of an empire into its lover's
arms.

A recruitment of hearsay,
undergirding the echoes, taken
for constant companions to
briefings on the silence that
endears.

Nestor's Day Off

Impromptu epics summing up a laundry list, with a long and winding journey into spontaneity. A sea at victory. Emissarial dinghies docking with overtures in the harbor of baffled screams for help. Kudos mumbled. Above as good as beneath the radar, culling in–betweeners from the swoosh of events on either side. The keys to flotation dangling from the belt loops of landlubbers, sprucing up the image of sinking into debt to shallow waters. Making peace with the hitching post in a town of horseless carriages. The brutal irrealities joining hands in appreciation of the undeniable, supplying the suburbs with the will to go on.

Big

Between the realities, old men toss horseshoes. The colossus settles into its easy chair like a dancing bear into the arms of Ginger Rogers, lending common coin to bon vivants in the bistro of dreams. Don't fly when walking will do. As pitiable geometry takes shape for a stroll. Turn, turn, turn of the century. But curiously really is enough. The Rambler started down the road to immaculate declensions. Easily stunted in waiting for the next to shed its skin. The movie where everybody dies in the manner to which they are accustomed. A comedy of petroglyphs leaves the cold world laughing. The beauty, of what might never have been, astounds even the cross eyed librarian. Brought to bear the brunt of history's tango boggling trophies from the sky. Caressing like a lullaby at the starting line of the human race.

Buridan

Simultaneous serendipities halving babies on D–Day, of the calendar counting days for what they're worth in Hong Kong. The crackers Polly killed for. Avenues through which the pain drives a limousine, as time expires in the arms of its demon lover. A nominal down payment of mutterings into the microphone on behalf of children everywhere. Fitting proportions to the purchase of warmth. The quack before the duck. Holding on to the *verboten* for dear life, for fear of fear that fear will lead to nowhere. Jesus baseball slice of Norman Rockwell pitching causes for the holes in a life raft of casual attire. A hippodrome for horses in wheelchairs, echoing with the applause of spiritual amputees, desperately muffling expressions of their love for cotton candy. Contexts leaning inward towards the luxury of feeling round.

Colloquial Patter

The incredulous belief, in the tingling of toes at land's end, lures scuba divers into the wading pool of easy recipes for lunch. Salami on peace on earth. A blur of sympathies freezing time. Redolent, for distance brewing. The tiki rooms in Zanzibar take Venus to Willendorf and back again. Light is cheap. A lay down in the tall grasses. Homeboy stripped of epaulettes. The lurking keeps the captain company. As erstwhile heroes of the daily grind commit consensual perjury at the altar of the winking nod. Braided in crawl, where you will find, without ever having to look. Drab armor modeled by nudes in the light that addles for posterity's sake. Visceral transparencies tuning last month's violin. A dilution of the toxins teaching history in the round. The beached whale takes up gardening. As the peace rages, the war blows dreams out of proportion, to the beneficence of the legless holding hostages in a secrecy of all the good places to run.

Death in Life

The equivocally threatened loss of membership, in the fraternity of huddled wildebeests, chanting mantras in counterpoint to the laughing of lions in the grass. Incumbent odors of the remains of a grand hypothesis, blindly charging deep into the conundrum of tall orders. Pinhole's moment in the sun. The tempo estranged. Faces fresh from practice at looking terribly pleased, at the first appearance of boomerangs on the horizon. Brussel sprouts in the recipe for manna. The squawk of parrots in the rafters of a bona fide delusion, making the rounds of the talk show circuit, like a warm fuzzy reminder of the smell of a blue haired matriarch's Sunday bath in rosewater. The triumphal procession of chosen moments, amply girded for the collision with memory. Murmurs saddled to an eclipse. A rhythm of tire irons on aluminum, herding future Olympians down alleys of queasy choice. The sycophants squealing like chinchillas at the coming of the lord from below.

Counting Around

Quintillion times askance to
oblique the angle taken, as a way
to prove zero to itself. Round in
the cheeks and heavy in the hips.
A goose egg in a hunt for
something taller.

An exponential childhood freckled
with feigned regret, as a way to
salvage fingers and toes from the
fire. Glommed in pose and frozen
in chase. A vapor sustaining a
craving for water.

Unfinished

A tutelage of ventriloquists throwing their voices into the sea, biting into the luxury of a last chance to taste old realities. Sureties of salt, remedies for naught's best chance at redemption in the world of whole numbers. A troll, an ogre and an elf, but not necessarily in that order. Dilettantes determined to make a difference, in the cost of lethargy to the thrill of floating by. And yet claustrophobia remains a favorite hobby, in the end that is the end of what you will it wouldn't but it does. Cherry picked width of the chasm at the point of no return. The sensuality of reverter clauses, stacked to make a mockery of quintessences, worn like earrings to the funeral of daylight. Lassoing the most silvery of moons in their haunting dreams. As if it were all that easy, getting an equity loan from the blood bank. Getting mononucleosis from the rumor of a protagonist at large.

Near

Not too far from where is how that when came time for shrinking violets. A handsome solitude takes a mirror in for repairs. Slurred tangents of quicksilver, jealous lampshades, a lonesome criteria making light from leftovers. Where near is dear to distance yielding dividends their ghosts. Naked as Halloween. Imperiled by shadow, gruff dusk. The quicksand of rocket science belches mysterious odors, into knapsacks that porters carry on and off the train. The jimmy crack corn of caribou tippy hoofing through eggshells of summer. Fire retardant kindling, bursting into a laughter of snaps and crackles. Fugue states are neither red nor blue, but colors rendered moot by the coming of nighttime, drawn by children with crayons they trust to cure polio. A shaving cream of smithereens lathers the b that a can c. Beauticians eat the foie gras. The bloat of loyal yeomen provide ballast for the histrionics of specks on the horizon. Popeye rows the boat ashore.

Cliff Diving

The shape of things to come as you are. The iridescent arc, of the salamander's leap from the cold passion of the cave, building bridges meeting water halfway. Concisely statuesque. The mollycoddlers, in their paisley mumus, consensually rising like turbid floodwaters, in grievous allegiance to the wholesome charm of the long missing link. The swift courses in algebra, leaving the boat people to grasp at logarithms. A house of common gestures. As you rise above an upbringing, to sink that serpentine putt on the 18th hole of a Russian novel. An intermission in the gravity of existence. The penultimate, if only this once.

Fathoms

Smoke, as told in prose. Aqueous, the sound of a tree falling for the forest's charms. A hand in the war footage dangling at the holster. Quiet's doublespeak encrypting valentines. A thirst, as it backstrokes on fortunate riptides. Naked for the fashion show of gestures harvesting corn. Taking pause from the shelf life, lived in waiting for candor in the objects held dear. Twinkles in the hiccup of wide open spaces. Deputies in the saga of every man for himself. The presumption of portals in a gaze upon the clandestine, the something for all to see.

Keeping It

Simplicity's adjutant sporting a fig leaf to the cotillion. A malleable antidote to what ails ya, when the bacterium come storming the gilded gates. Mesothelioma in the pestiferous trenches. Genetically altered tulips, everywhere. A casual alabaster of newt's belly, complementing a collage of charities. The turbulence varnished to baroque. Exit ramps repealing the right to merge: a lawnmower with a fine tooth comb attempting to straighten things out. Bring milk and honey together, in a mud wrestle delighting audiences af all ages. A savage arrested by a bright light (you see) your mother kissing a Martian and then it happens. To adjudicate a slickened slope of an ice storm, the gray light of perfection burning like plutonium on the horizon. A vibrato of little nothings. The orotund retorts to the precarious balance of objects on the shelf, daring the earth to shake the leaves to surrender. The contiguous meatgrinder to take a moment from the cookie jar, and hold it up for the aging matador to see.

Cover

Naked leprechauns making news in the world of basketball. The speed of light in a school zone. The crux of parallels, illustrating a crossroads at the blind school for those deafened by a belief in noise. Silhouetted certainties stepping out of range, of the voyeur's shot in the dark night of faces grown pumpkinesque with shadow. The reluctant reliance on lugubrious overtones to laugh. A reciprocal gratitude for services rendered inoperable, a self–reflexive grief at the sound of bells, setting the belfry in the foreground of an anecdote defusing a time bomb on the courthouse steps. The repellant qualities of various glues, sticking in the mind of a slow practitioner. The gold bullion of cow dung in a garden of leafy greens, absolving the mayor from his oath to urban planning. A winter frieze of ice nymphs barbecuing angels in the snow. The varnish on the doublespeak of the birds.

Profile Cabinet

A wheeze of factoids cramming life into a nutshell, sixth sense of purpose snuffing the candle on the cake of eaten too. Relics of nuance sequestered for clarity. Righted alibi sifting anecdotes for circulation in the swimming pool. Scent of collectibles lost on the letterhead of Dear John's keepsake. A misdemeanor of adjectives buckling the knees on great events, encapsulated for consumption by prisoners of a to z. Broadened sighs filling a brown paper bag with a decade of struggles in the eerie. Minutes distilled to whom.

The Birth of Etcetera

Some days I'm not in the mood
for my raincoat. The hobble out
to the woodshed I've become.
Token of a myopic mysticism,
entranced by cinderblocks and
lipstick scrawled in Sanskrit
forging bonds of gooey clay.
Graffiti on the walls of the
inscrutable. Every now and
when I see a cartoon laugh of
jackals haunting an echo of old
shoes. A stubborn collage of
noises unmeant to turn a head
to think. To dally in a cocoon
of circles assured of dying
light of fires in the holes that
bring the mountains round
as well.

Silhouettes

It was snowing in Alabama, not here, in the aftermath. A sense of rooted tumbleweed, fostering an illusion of castles on a horizon of purple skies, generously plastered across the Milky Way at twilight. A panoramic contour to the course of canceled events. Gilded lilies, chastened with hint of winter's creep up legs to Goshen. Not here, the weather on standby. An icy evocation of tears, for dollars spent doctoring the dead in the kitchen. Subject to the tall orders of the beehive coiffure, manning kiosks at the gates to heaven, as hunchback plumbers come running with the water into a picture of the flood of the humanity. But easily seen from here, the front porch of a reason to believe. The terwilligers of convolution with immensities to trespass, before time moves on to ellipses consoling mothers in the haberdashery. A constellation of events recorded in the touch the skin takes to bone for safekeeping. Steps taken off the continental shelf in procession to dance's doorstep, making the turn into the homestretch a metamorphosis of which everyone can be proud. Footprints in a cursive of cold toes. Echoes trimmed to a Morse Code of bumps in the night, setting the tempo on a pedestal of rosewood.

Do

Blood pressure the children to behave

Subordinate a boarding pass go to jail

Feel the pain with clean fingers, easily
pointed in any direction you choose

Filibuster one last cry for help from
the sole survivor

Attend a meeting of the mind your
manners of the masters of chiaroscuro

Numb the intuition of the hesitant
keeping time with manufactured
premonitions

Mock the premise of making peace
with the residuum of morning

Eat spaghetti, from strings of theory

Deduce the paradoxical origin of
minutemen, from the hour that
is always with us

Lean To

Window No. 3. Approximate accommodations for the comfortably lost. A sabbatical pigeonholed in a bus schedule, an error in the trajectory of sunlight, a protagonist as he takes that first, all telling step into the foyer. A rustic profile to a manmade lake of crocodile tears. Whereas the roster was always full of applicants, doorknockers from the old school, the childhood mysteries of 42nd Street, bundled up in myths curbing urban darkness on the high noons of bare feet in the park. Third door to the left of where you were standing when. The walls came calling. The yellowed rainbows scarred a wedding picture. The color blue was sent out holding hands with an arpeggio, promoting raw contours to the landscape, sculpted for the aesthetic purview of no one necessarily near. It could have been any of a number of people, sharing silhouettes with the doppelgangers of a moment's notice. Yet another face in the window. Another friend to feed the news.

Here

A belated misanthropy tossing taunts at the manhood of Mona Lisa. A license to ignite candles, extended beyond a belief in warmth. Blind men bluffing eagle eyes into setting their sights too low. Buried in altitudes of ivory. Word trickling down to gossip on the commodities market, as little piggy goes. In creasing the hat brim to fit the head of the sandman, poking into the business of the beyond. A scratching noise at the rear of a moratorium. Rudiments of the infinite compounding into something simply small. The unstoppable contagion of laughter, spreading influenza like butter on a biblical drone of little nothings. Brute caresses pounding strokes of luck, into the formula for success in falling into hammocks of understanding. Crunching the numbers game into fractions of the cost of knuckles, clustered into voting blocs throwing weight as ante to the war, for mindful hearts beating as one change of clothes into the comfort of cotton. A shrill holler out the screen door, amplified in taking summer to task for its sponsorship of the withering. Salting down adages for the long bus ride into town. As if unscathed by the drowning points of old imaginations. A history of mysteries queued to form a noose around the neck of a certain someone. Wiling away the miles in homage to the ingenuity of the wheel.

The Air

The miasma going good with salt
Pretzel's lost lover in the loop
A big shot in the foot of yarn the cat will chase to glory day
Years on the assembly line of body parts
Purple hearts pulsing
Figment's chime
Undone as doing's blessing
Resolved
Cabana boy hats
The plush fur of living examples
Paralysis at the speed of lightweights lifting truncheons from poverty
The scores to be tallied in retrospect
Cues to perform where best your oboe will find an audience
Arrearage in the bold step
The family fossils
Penury of gobbledygook at the juncture of thesis and bride

Now is Here

Deep fried coagulants stall traffic,
in sacred heart school Five drachmas please
Three swinging doors to your left...the other, the other left
Pitiably jutted jaw launching ambushes on imported turf

Amateur anglers pitching tents, as far as they would fly
into the footnotes Victory at sea
The arctic pains, where ice is king 13 o'clock
Tall grass is the next to go Tawdry curriculum pervades
the slobbered utterance spawned over coffee and smoke

A police force is what you make of it
A calliope and a library lip
No, the tainted olives won't succumb to the rites of passage,
the furtherance of the lesser for the most part

That's for what's left to say
The lemon trees posturing as canopies
The forthright burying cousins in the yard
Immaculate mud bath The gondoliers
are coming The multiple choice questions are gone

Dulcet

A vigorous polyphony and then. Juxtaposed in solitude. An inch from a mile after mile. Run. Toward. Waiting capsizes, and the scuba divers find a sense of purpose. Depth, where water is vulnerable. Wizened toadies backstroke for posterity's wreath, only to find. A tympani of touchés. A hopeless glimmer. Two notches on a stick, just above the mean tide. The various meets the sundry at high noon. Impossible meets the standard, by which the weather is judged competent, to rule the moods of the postman. The lugubrious frown on the clown, on the postage stamp, stuck to its guns. The toll booths ring. What's what is rarely where it should be, but what's not is ensconced, on the wall that is the the wall of which the bridge builders whisper. The sweetness of nothings, purged of saccharine, in the corridors where echoes pay a toll. Where the shallows bristle, at a voice from beneath the breath of a diva.

Plus

Forensic flea circus of honest Abes in toyland, making
Much of the little they know. A corroboration of constellations,
Determining the identity of flying objects;
The me when the I ends the discussion,
With a starry burst of flavor from the outer reaches.

The art of tying shoes to promises to walk.
Proving proof itself proves nothing, but to worry the elders
In their amber years it takes to get an education, in the
Sophistries of watching the leaves blow.

Correcting the assemblages in their assumptions
Of togetherness, when the indictments sprinkle the dandelion
Fields with a fullness of body causing the saints
To shiver in ther sarcophagi.
The blithering to make perfect sense, in saying so to speak
In Rome, by way of saying each eye knows what the shadow
Means behind the curtain.

Now and Then

Permian red hair of the dog, sampled for fuel of blue angels blessing the fleet in the sand.
Polterzeitgeist ghost written epitaph.
A taste of success, on the slow ride into the remembrance of things to come.
Cautionary facades of failing granite.
Rubies in petals up the hill.
A premise of equality, between up and down in the spin cycle of the reasons, for men and women inured to running hot and cold.
As if nothing had happened.
An umbrage of green apples torturing natives with rules of godly azure.
A back and forth of surrenders to momentum, equivocal plateaus maintained for a season.
The sweet anesthesia of murder by proxy, that had never wafted in the breeze, in hymnal processions of well being aired for the neighbors to incorporate into their prayers for burgeoning coffers of corn.
A closet in the law of incredulity.
Wampum for ether.
An excerpt reinstated, by acclamation of other missing portions of the script.
Conundrums cut from whole cloth, being worn to a wedding of winking eyes on the bouncing ball, setting monsters free in the gloaming.

academy

Glottal ice cream pooling on the lips of teacher's pet in waiting. A caramel hyperbole assuaging the need to grow. A sweetness of nothings calibrated on stubby fingers, fresh from the loan of a hand to the man with the answer to nil. Lurking in authority over a rhetorical question, posed as a little boy in short pants mitigating the misdemeanors of the school day. The charter members of collaboration in the colors of the rainbow, wreaking crayon havoc in errant strokes of amnesty. The fruit of candlelight on the tree.

Simple

An illiteracy enveloping
gists of ineffable
inklings of rain. A
cumulative expanse of
blank parchment,
apologies for the wall
of tidings. Writing
wrongs. An ellipse with
a tablecloth.
Quagmires in an
alphabet, citing the
limitations of words to
the wizened at having
heard. An abandoned
scribble taming
gibberish for pony
shows in the gray light
eloping with sleep.

Sensible 2

Chasms illustrated with safety nets. A confusion of apprentice leapers, as to the extent to which falling furthers their quest for depth. The template for success in the coal mines. The heart of the colorist beating the tom toms wildly. Mauve light of August from Sears, where Mrs. Grumman's moustache killed a man once. A count to ten little frenzies taking a tantrum to jail. Undermining the ceiling with a celebration of the room below. The minty flavor of juleps in the air, translating Shakespeare into Javanese, for the patrons of the pending monsoon. The perfectly plausible quaintness of rituals, sustaining a numbness to the long drawn out thrill of it all. Why not vanilla? The cartographers moving mountains to lighten the load. But far be it is what it is. A sovereign monstrosity moonlighting as ubiquity, legislating the temperature of the room.

www.ingramcontent.com/pod-product-compliance
Lightning Source LLC
Chambersburg PA
CBHW020023050426
42450CB00005B/611